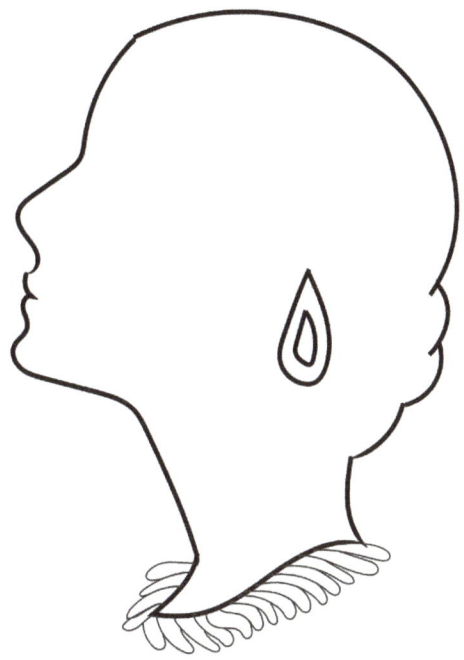

Entangled Beauties

Stay Beautiful by Coloring Your Stress Away

Author and Illustrator: Louie Cristine

Title: Entangled Beauties

ISBN: 978-1522953067

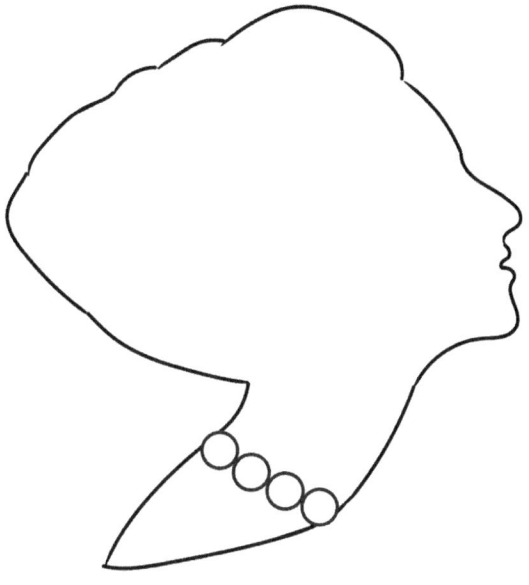

*This Book Belongs
to the Beautiful*

_____

To the most amazing woman in my life, my mom - Malou

To my greatest critic and supporter, my Baba - Mark

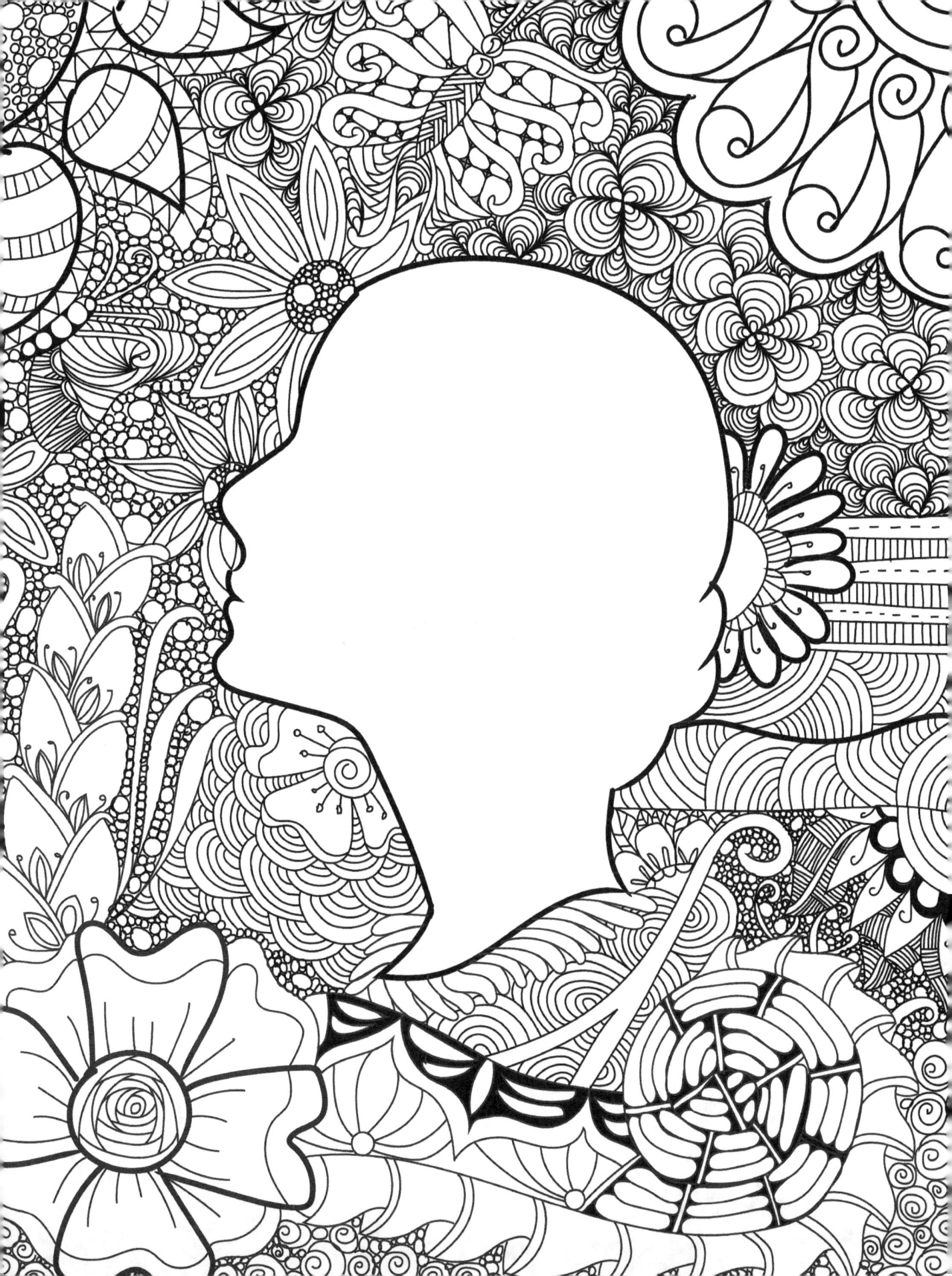

if YOU obey
all the RULES,
YOU MISS all the
FUN!

KATHARINE HEPBURN
AMERICAN LEADING LADY IN HOLLYWOOD
FOR MORE THAN 60 YEARS

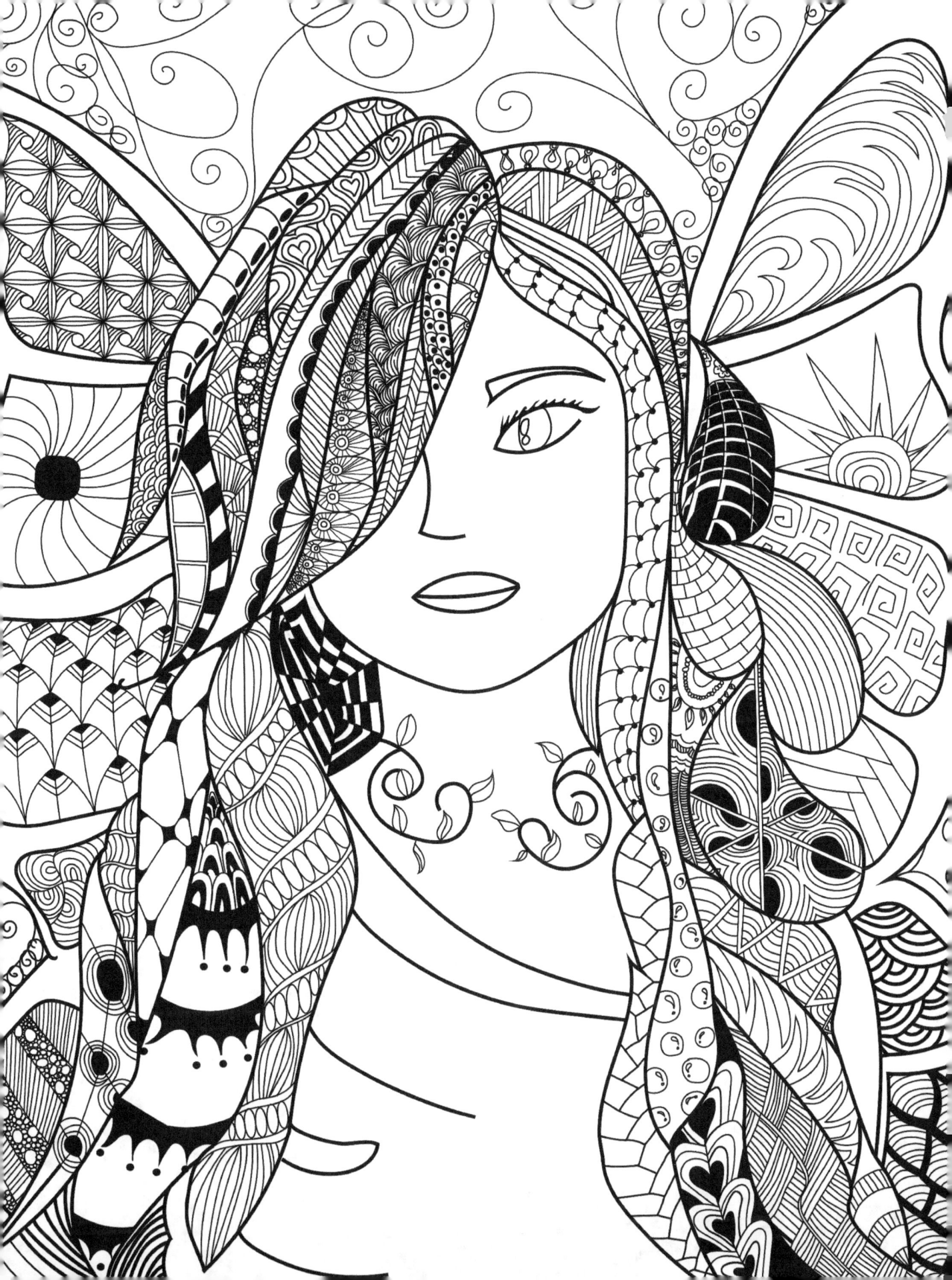

a WOMAN is like a TEA BAG

you never know how strong she is

until she gets in HOT water.

Eleanor Roosevelt
Longest-Serving First Lady of
the United States

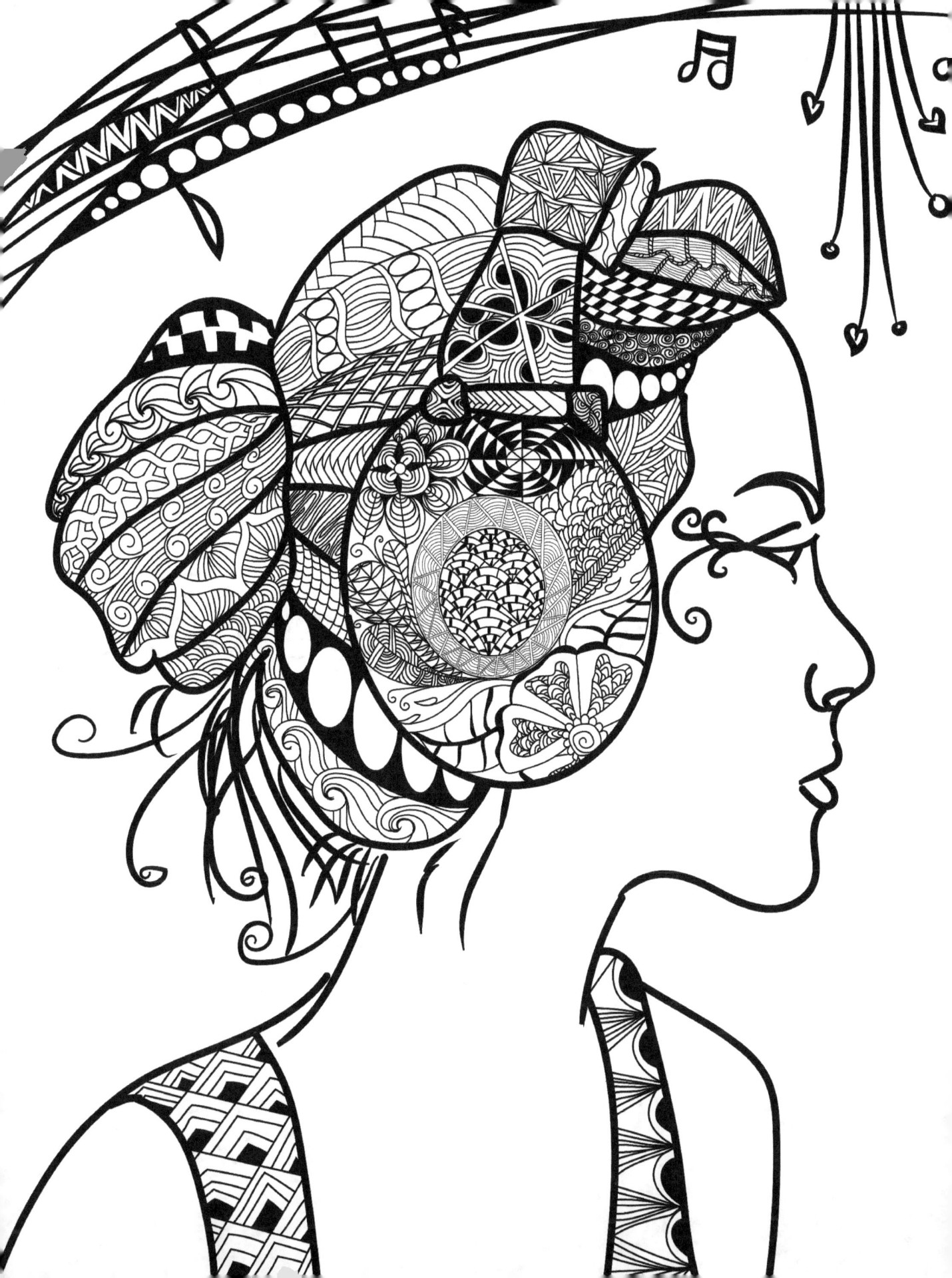

the BEST PROTECTION any WOMAN can have... is COURAGE.

ELIZABETH CADY STANTON
LEADING FIGURE OF THE EARLY WOMEN'S
RIGHTS MOVEMENT

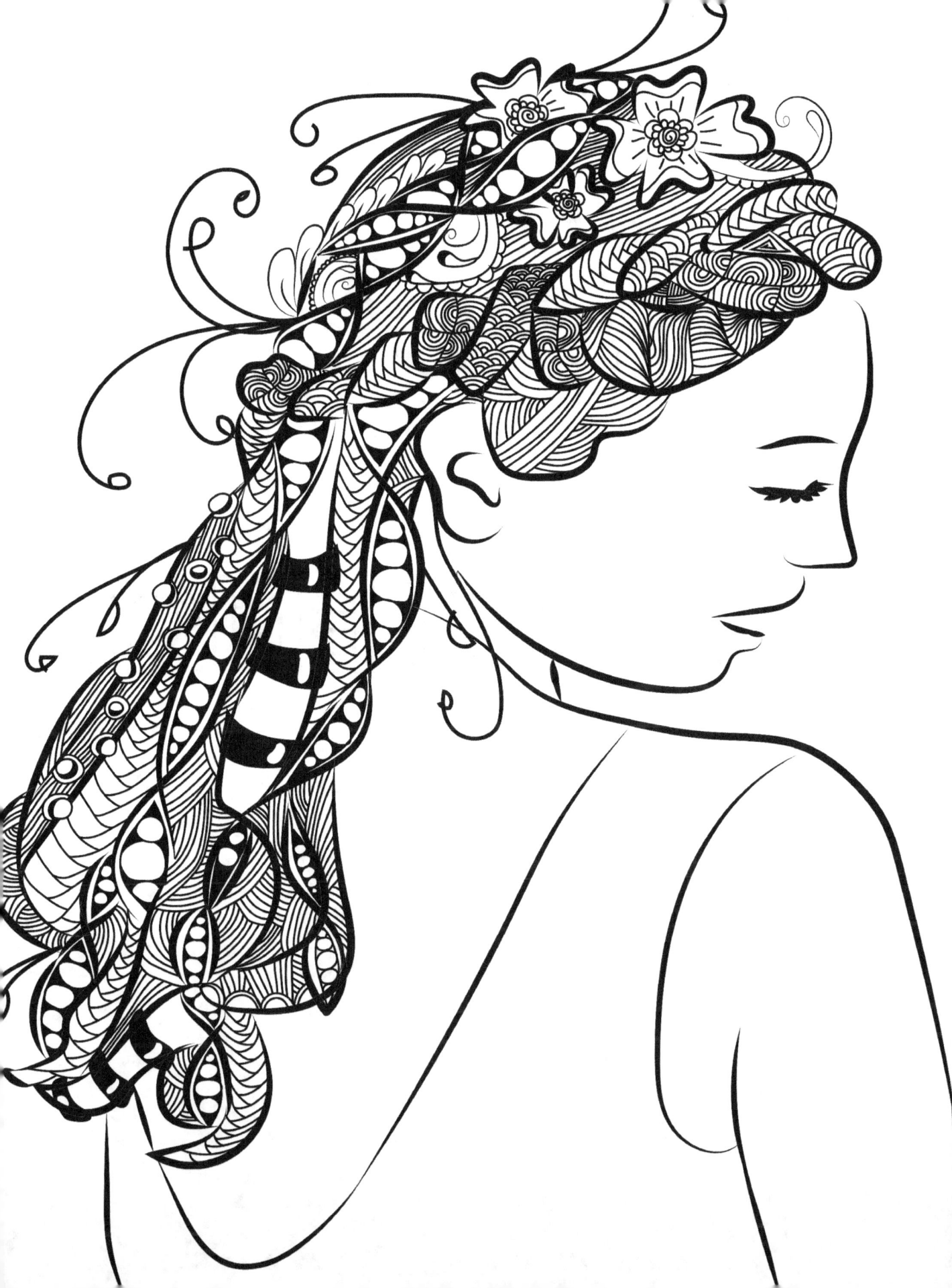

SUCCESS
breeds
CONFIDENCE

Beryl Markham
Writer, Pilot, Horse Trainer

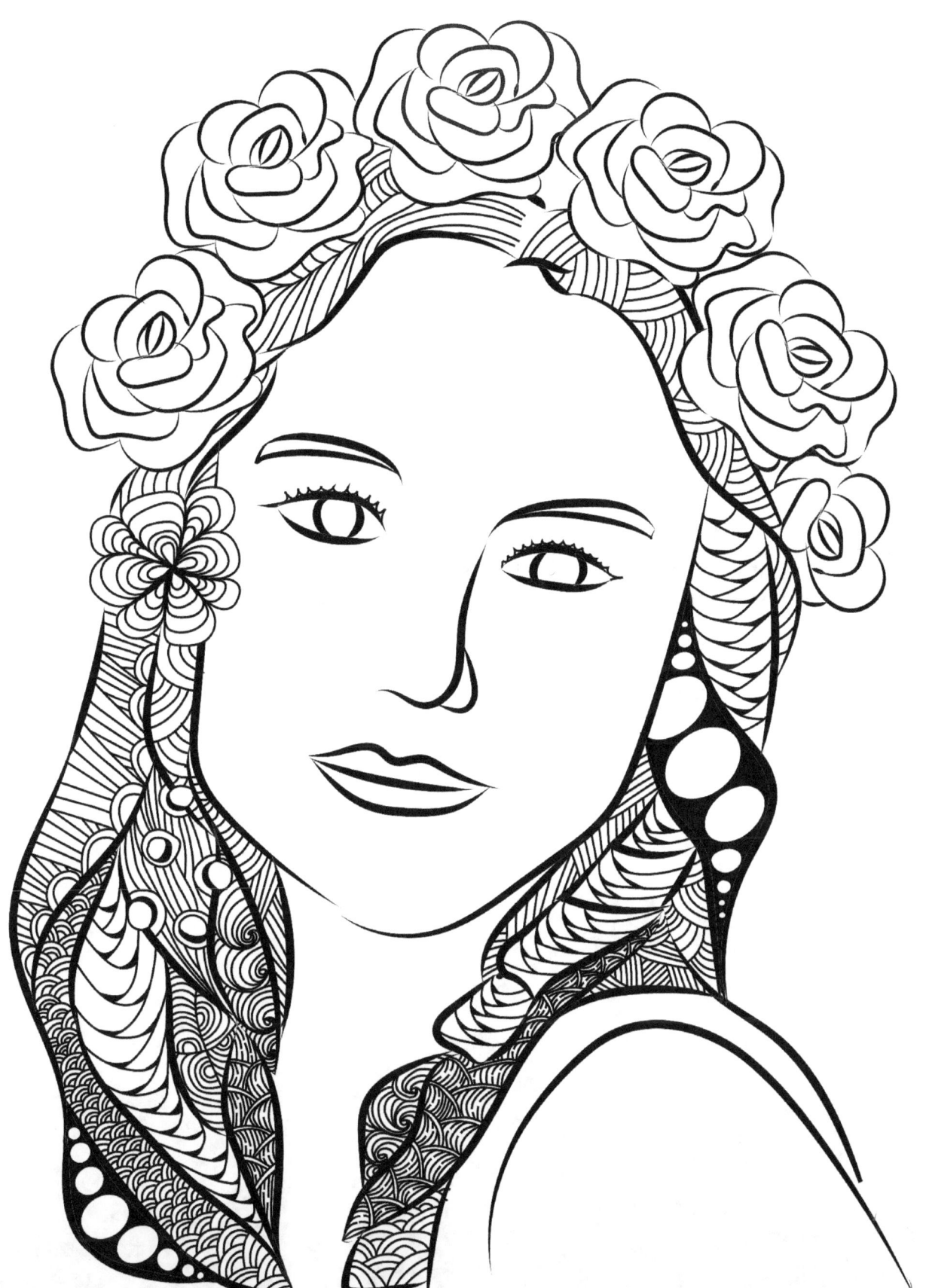

the question isn't WHO is going to let me; it's WHO is going to STOP me

AYN RAND
RUSSIAN-BORN AMERICAN NOVELIST,
PHILOSOPHER, PLAYWRIGHT, AND SCREENWRITER

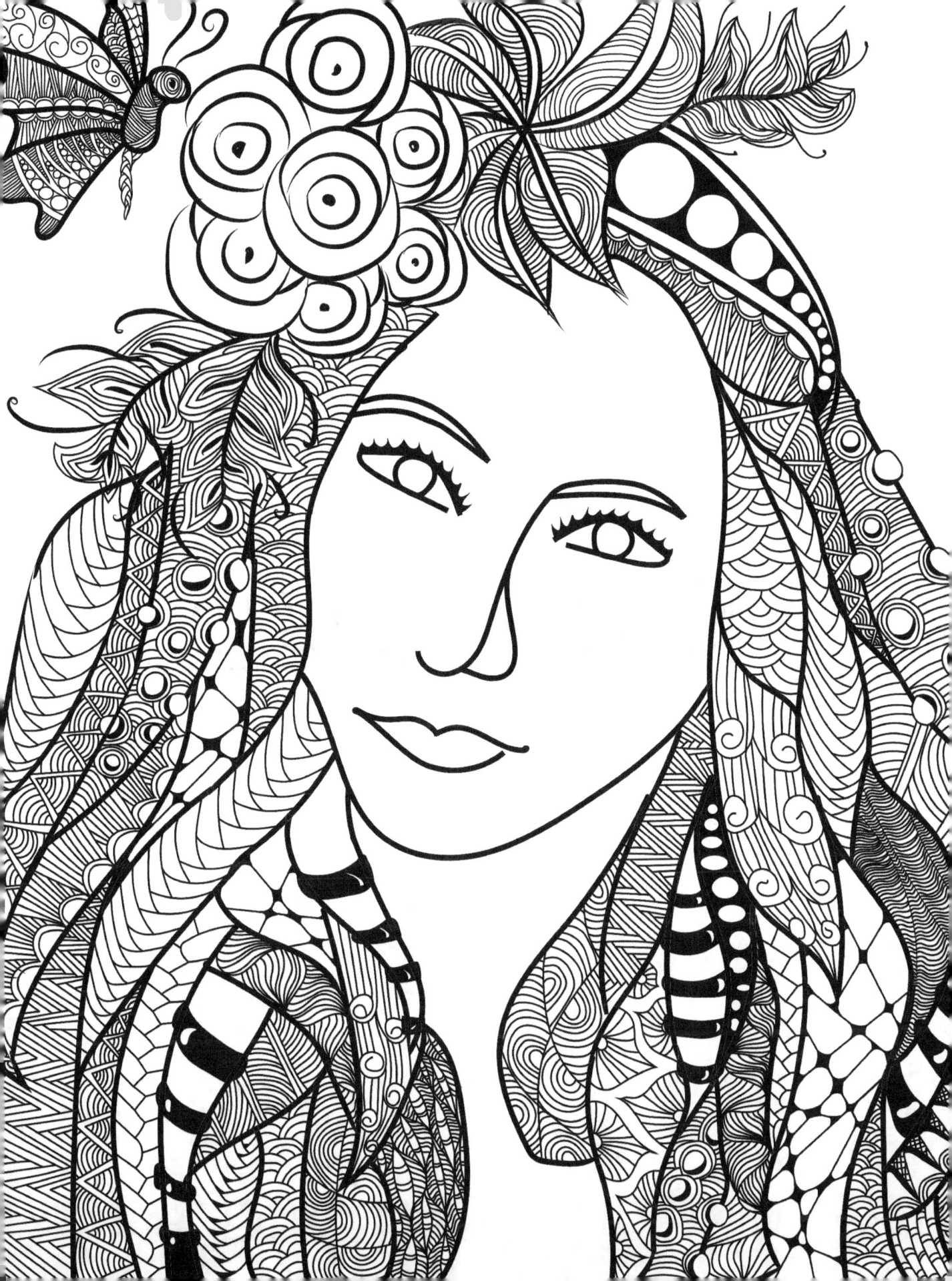

COURAGE is like a MUSCLE, we strengthen it by USE.

RUTH GORDON
American film, stage, and TV actress,
screenwriter and playwright

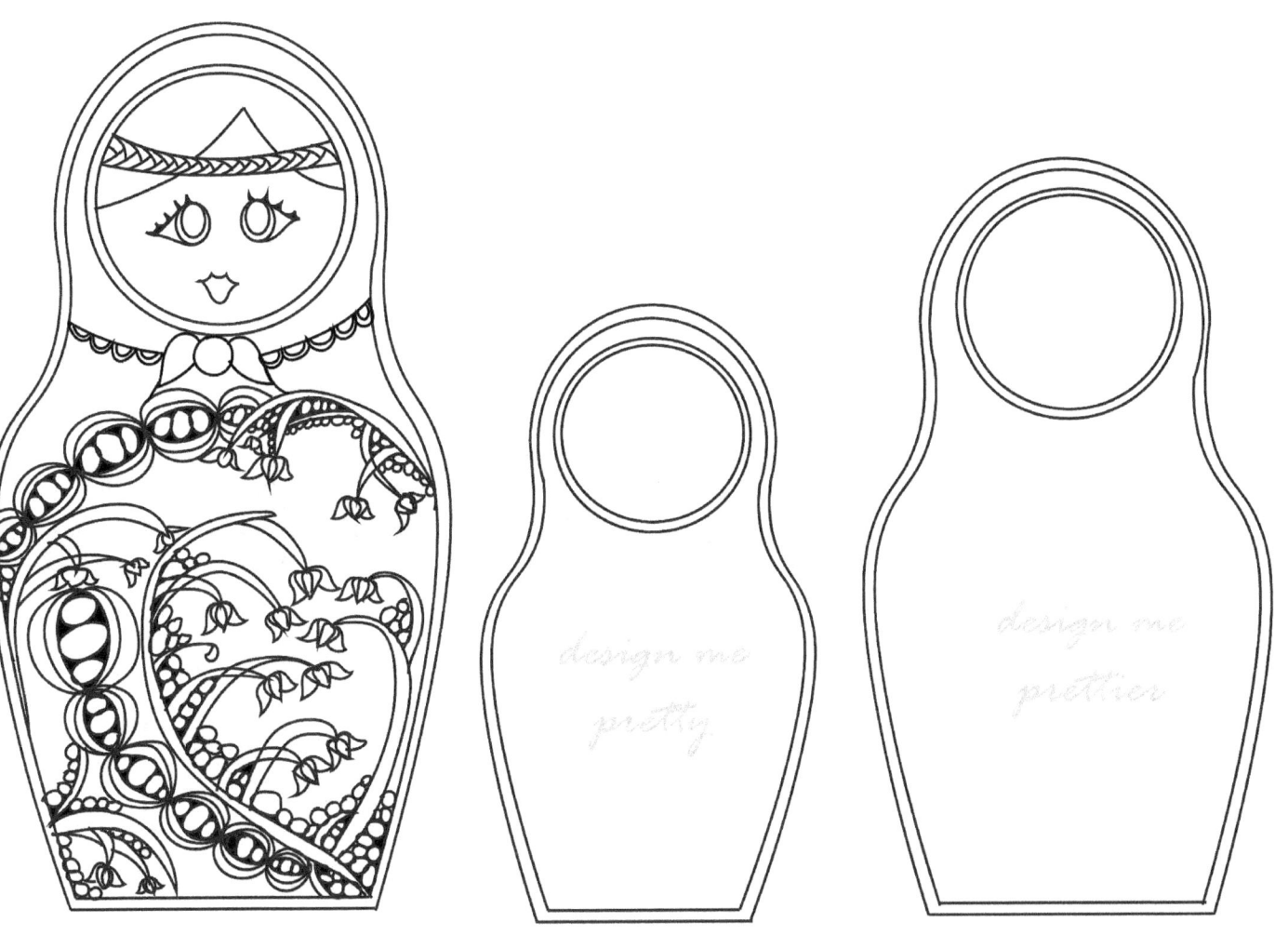

design me
pretty

design me
prettier

Option A is not available. so let's KICK the SH*T out of OPTION B.

SHERYL SANDBERG
COO OF FACEBOOK

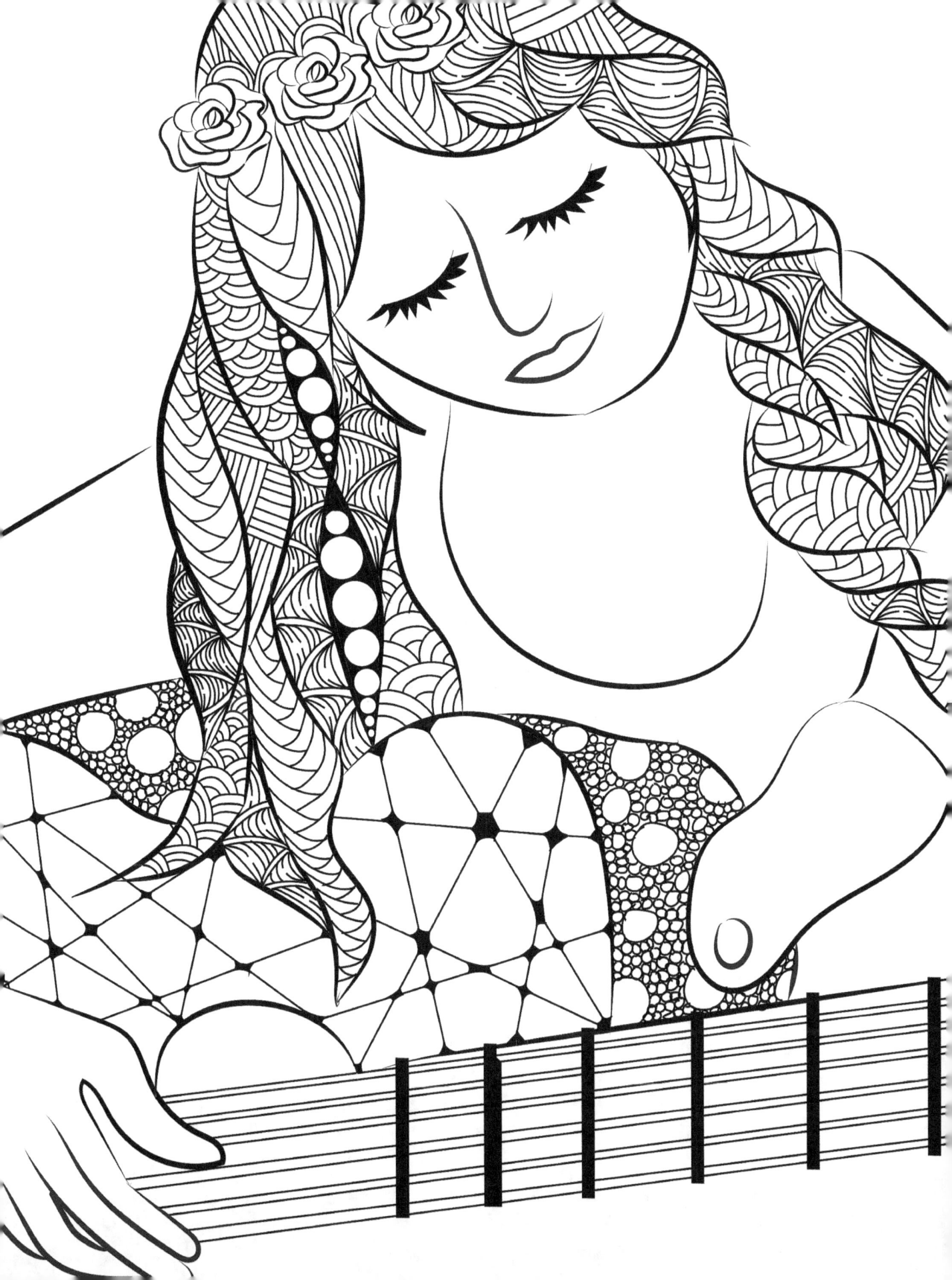

Dear Optimist, Pessimist, & Realist

- while you guys were busy arguing about the glass of wine,
I DRANK IT!
Sincerely, the Opportunist!

Lori Greiner
inventor, QVC host
and 'Shark Tank' investor

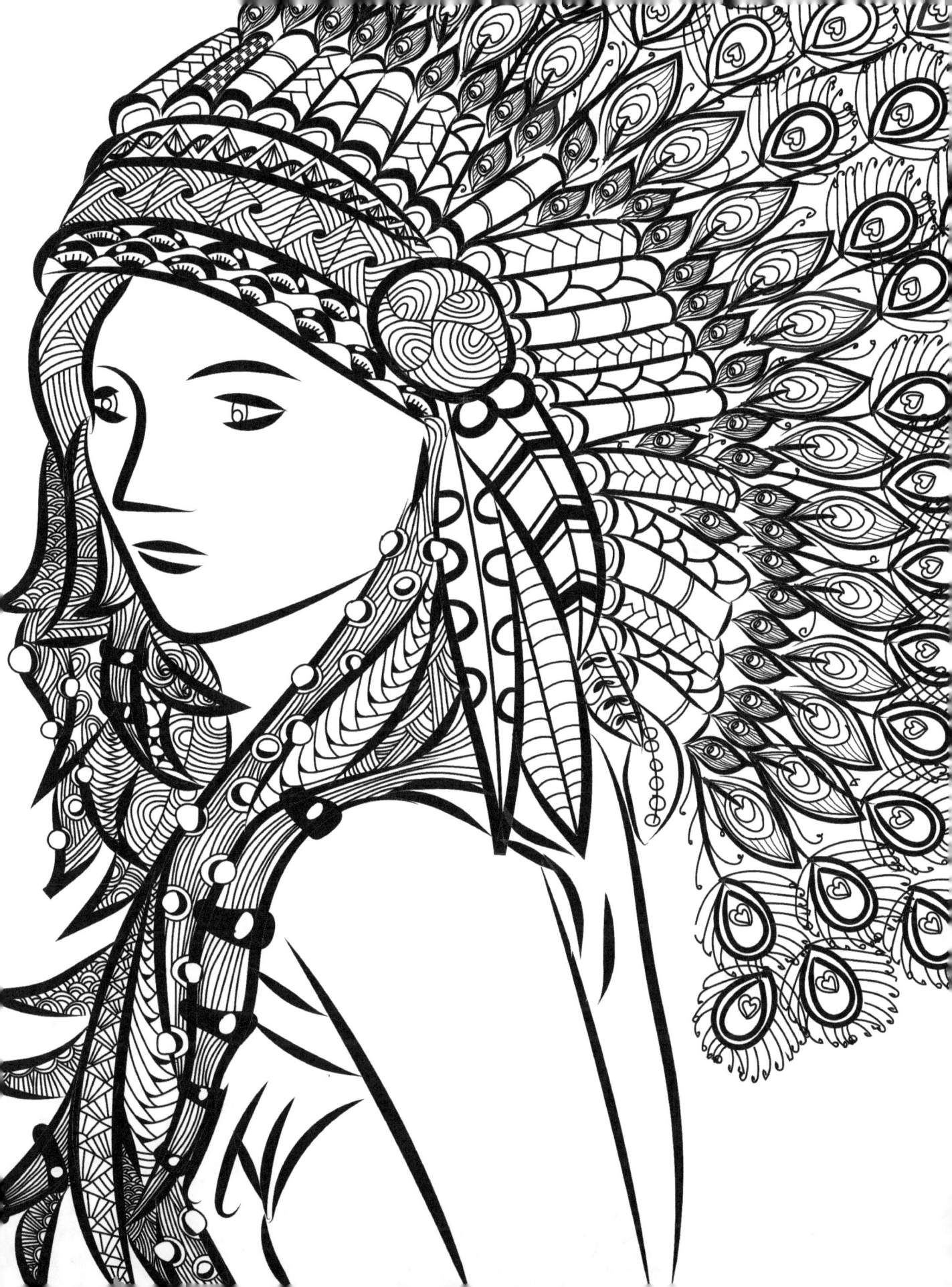

Aerodynamically, the BUMBLEBEE

shouldn't be able to fly, but the BUMBLEBEE doesn't know that so

it goes on flying anyway.

MARY KAY ASH
FOUNDER OF MARY KAY COSMETICS

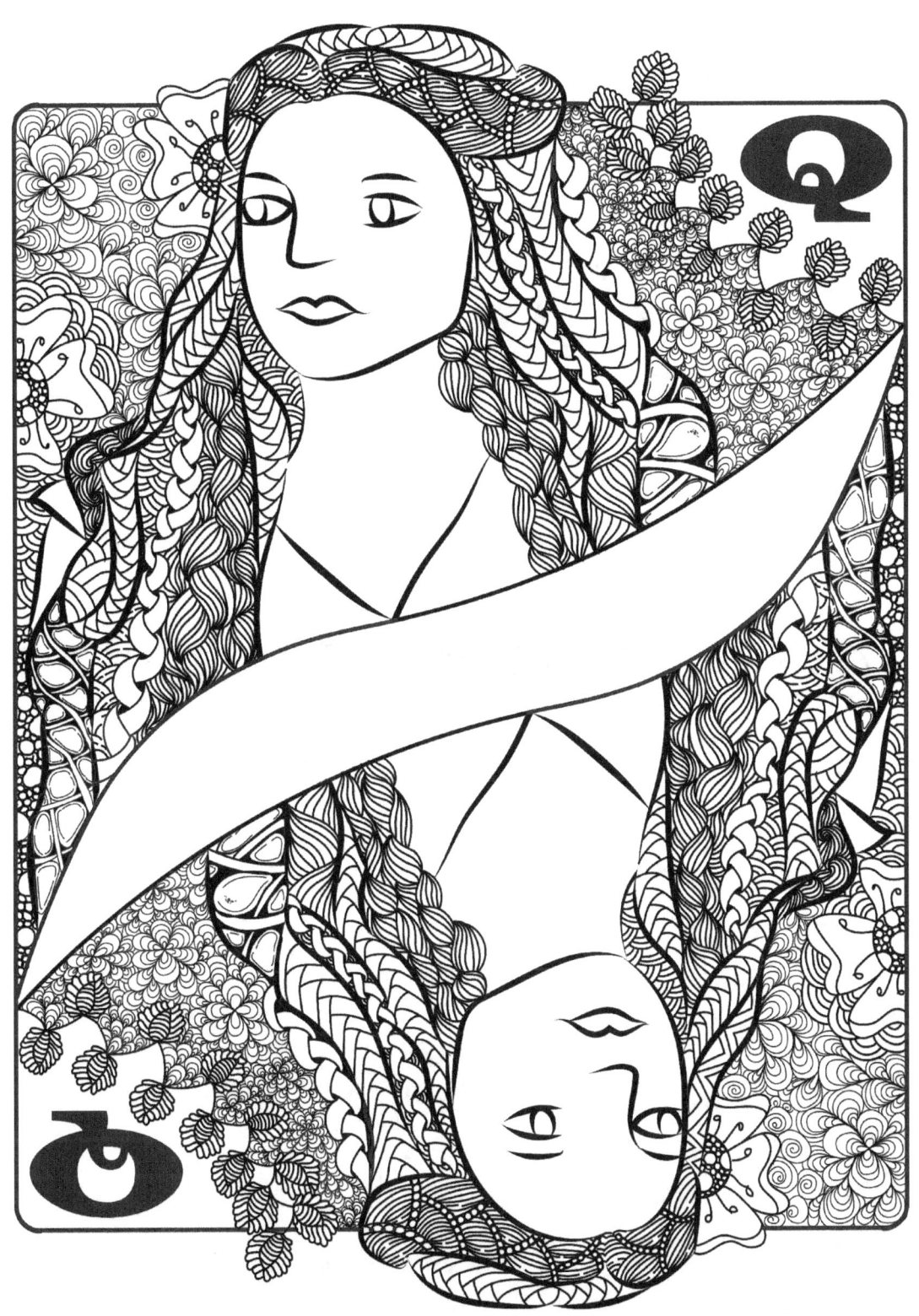

if I STOP to KICK every barking DOG, I'm not going to get where I'm going.

Jackie Joyner-Kersee
all-time greatest athletes in the women's heptathlon and women's long jump

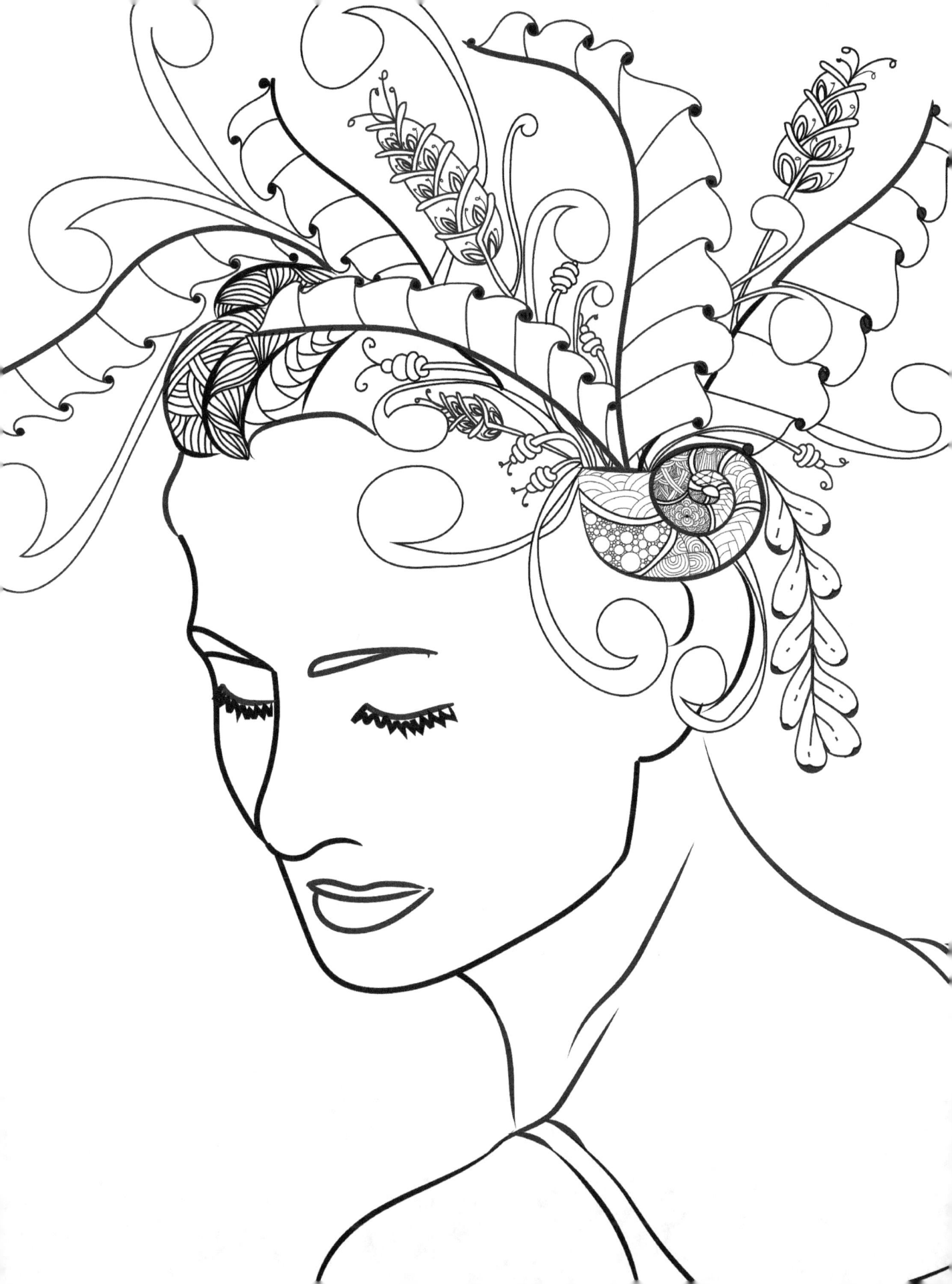

when the WHOLE WORLD

is SILENT, even one

VOICE becomes POWERFUL

Malala Yousafzai
Pakistani activist for female education
and the youngest-ever Nobel Prize
Laureate

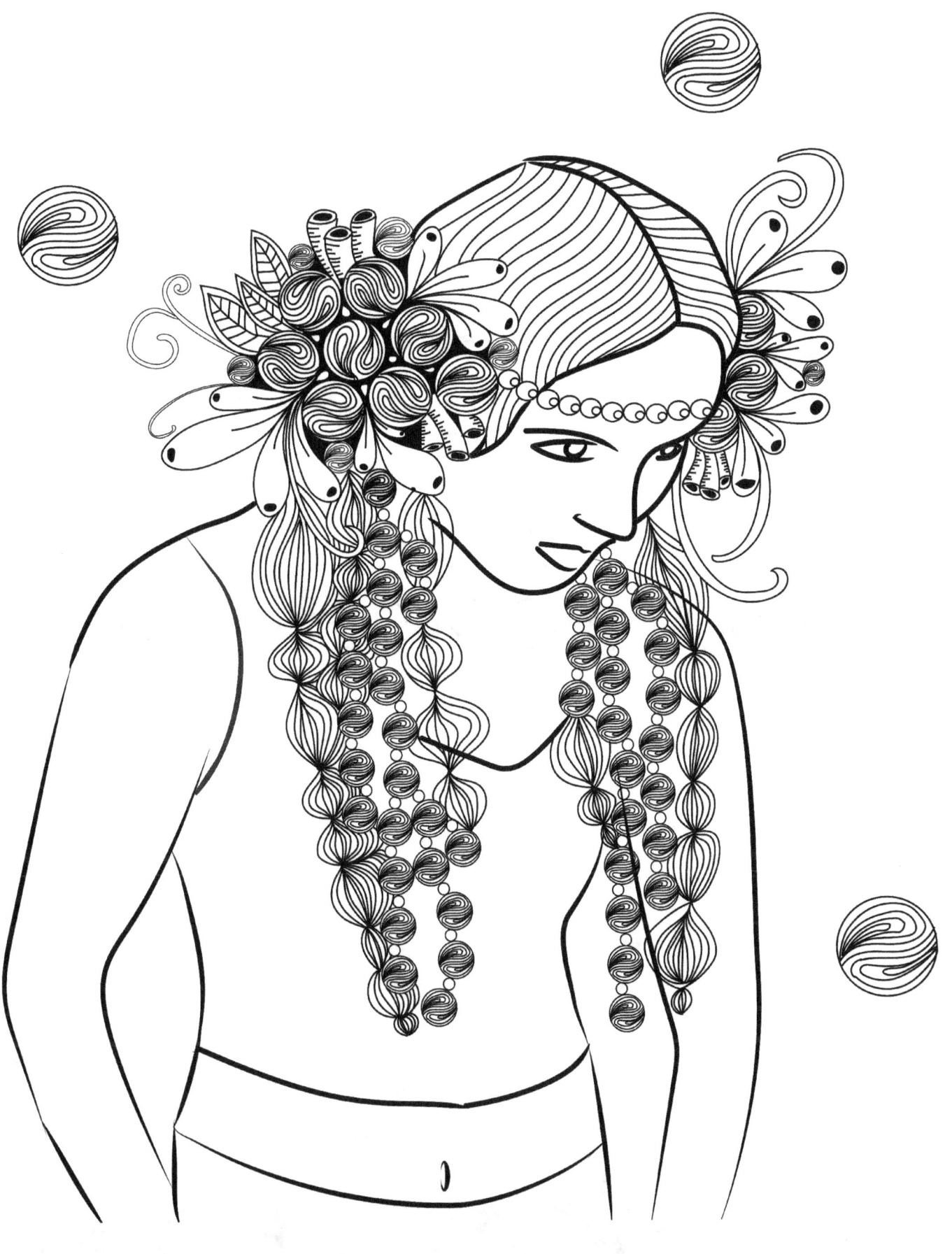

i DIDN'T get THERE
by WISHING for it,
or HOPING for it,
but by WORKING for it.

ESTée LauDer
CO-FOUNDER OF ESTée LauDer COMPANIES

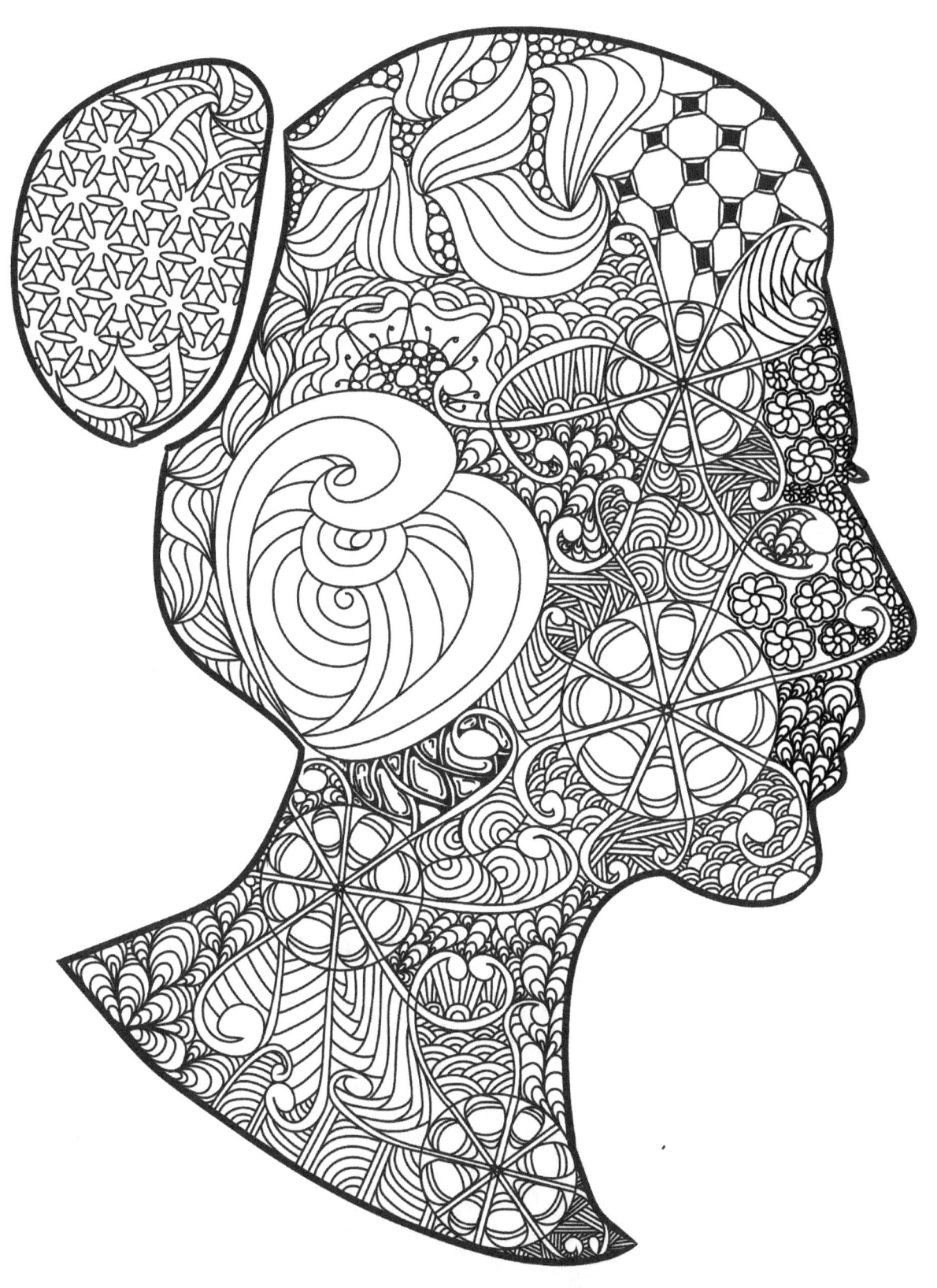

POWER is NOT given to YOU

You have to TAKE it!

Beyoncé Knowles
American singer-songwriter,
and actress

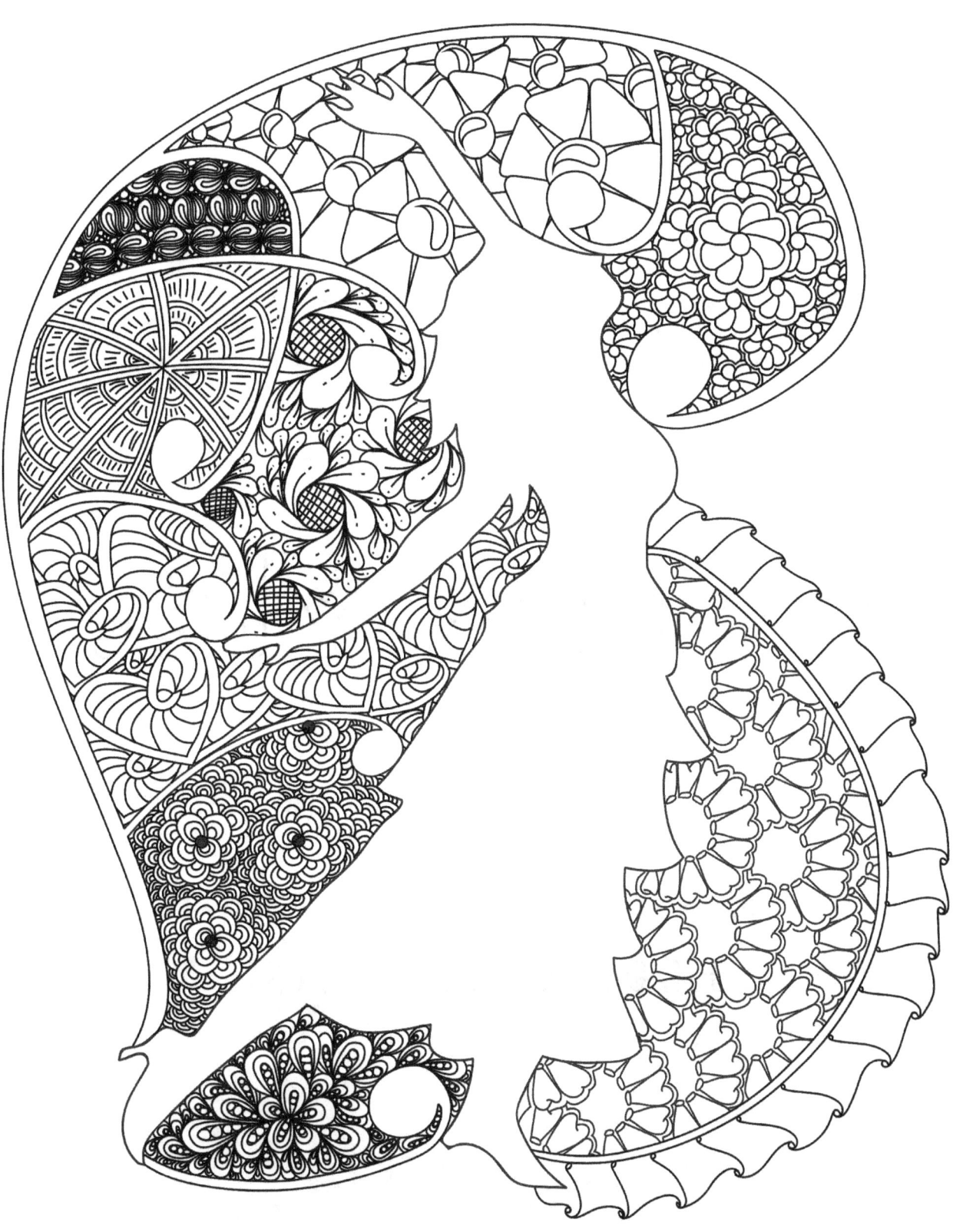

i have stood on a MOUNTAIN of NO's

for one YES.

B. SMITH
American restaurateur, model,
author, and television host

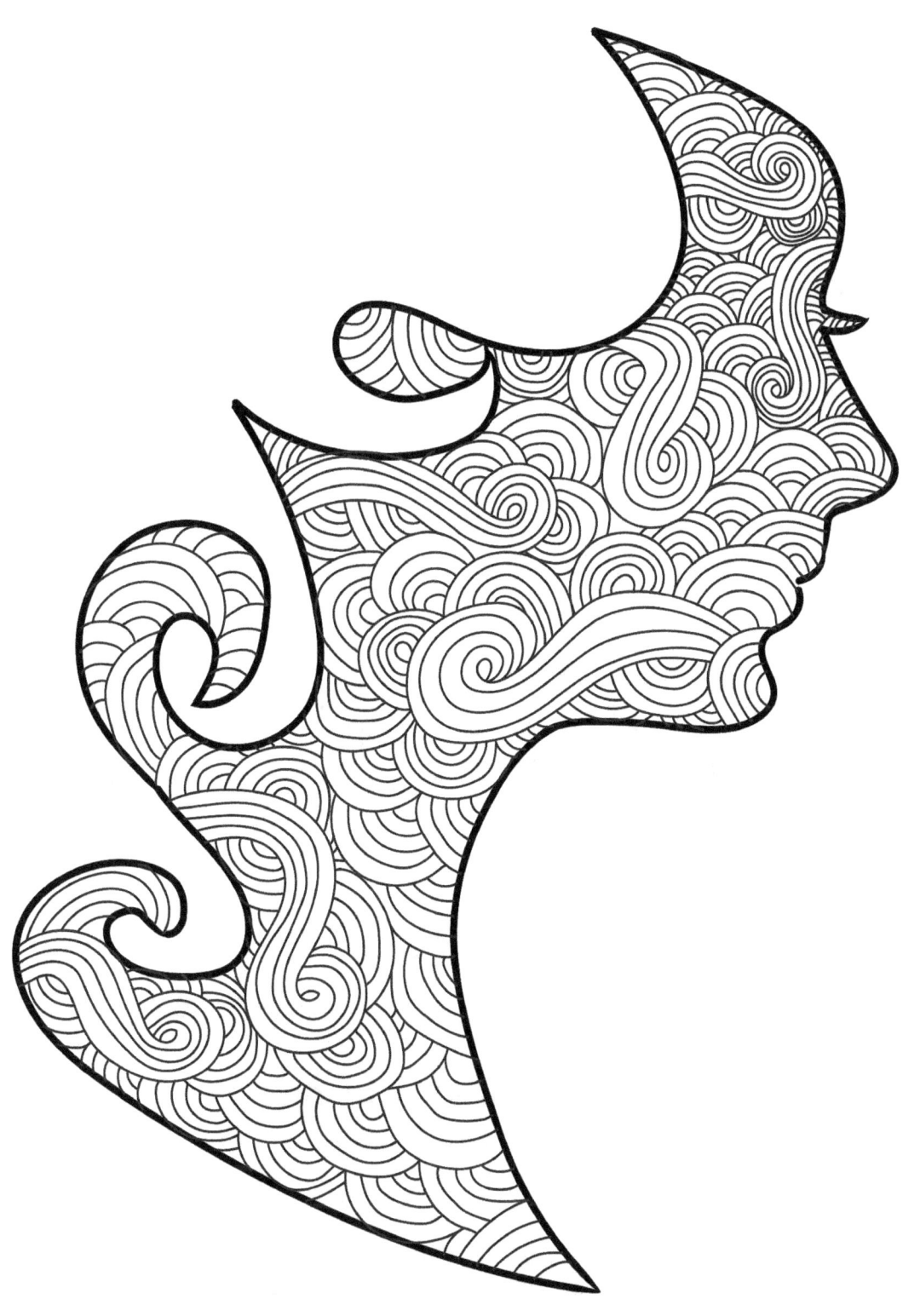

if YOU don't like the road
you're walking, START
PAVING another ONE

DOLLY PARTON
ACTRESS, AUTHOR, BUSINESSWOMAN,
AND HUMANITARIAN

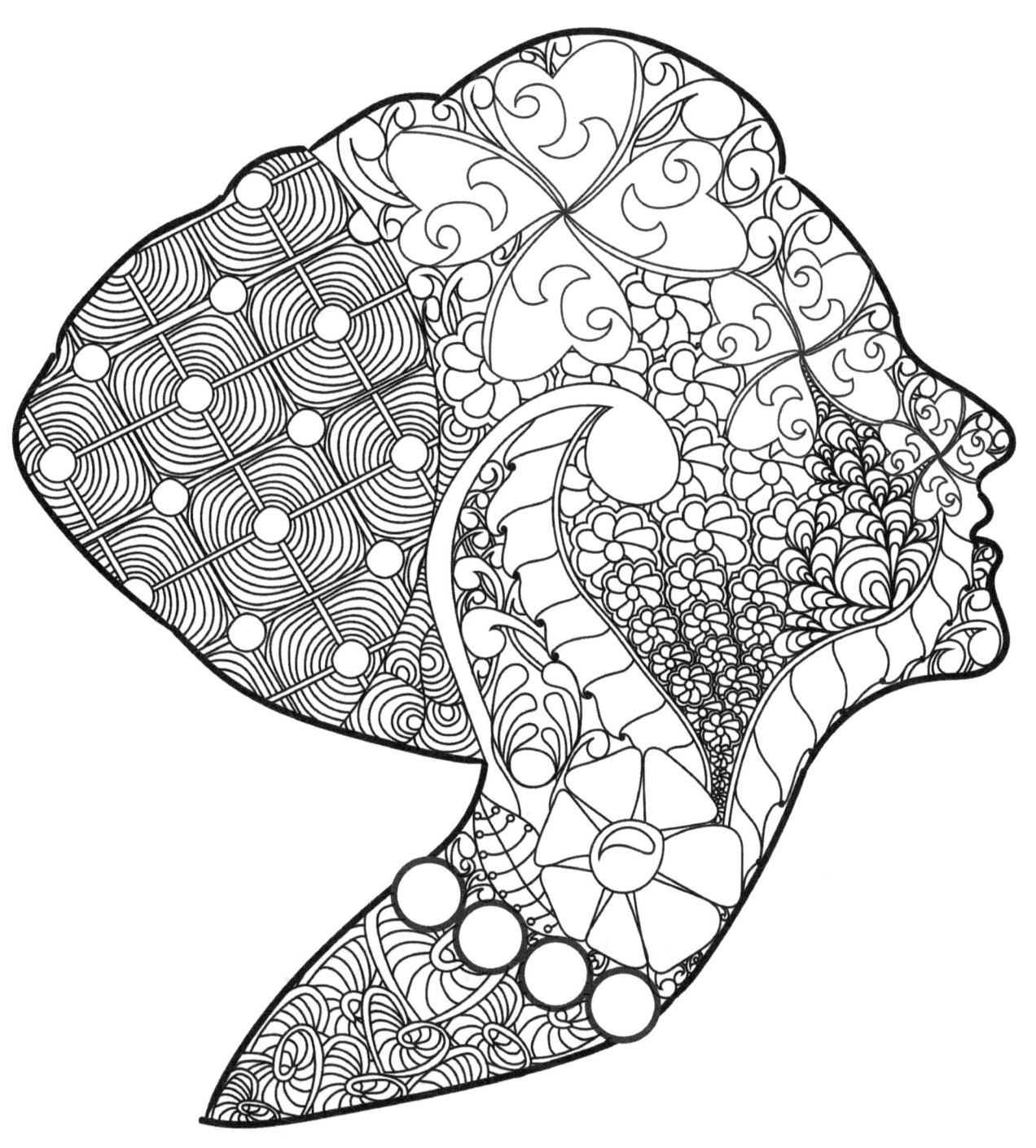

You CAN'T give up!
If you give up,
you're like
everybody else.

CHRIS EVERT
WORLD NO. 1 PROFESSIONAL TENNIS PLAYER
FROM THE UNITED STATES

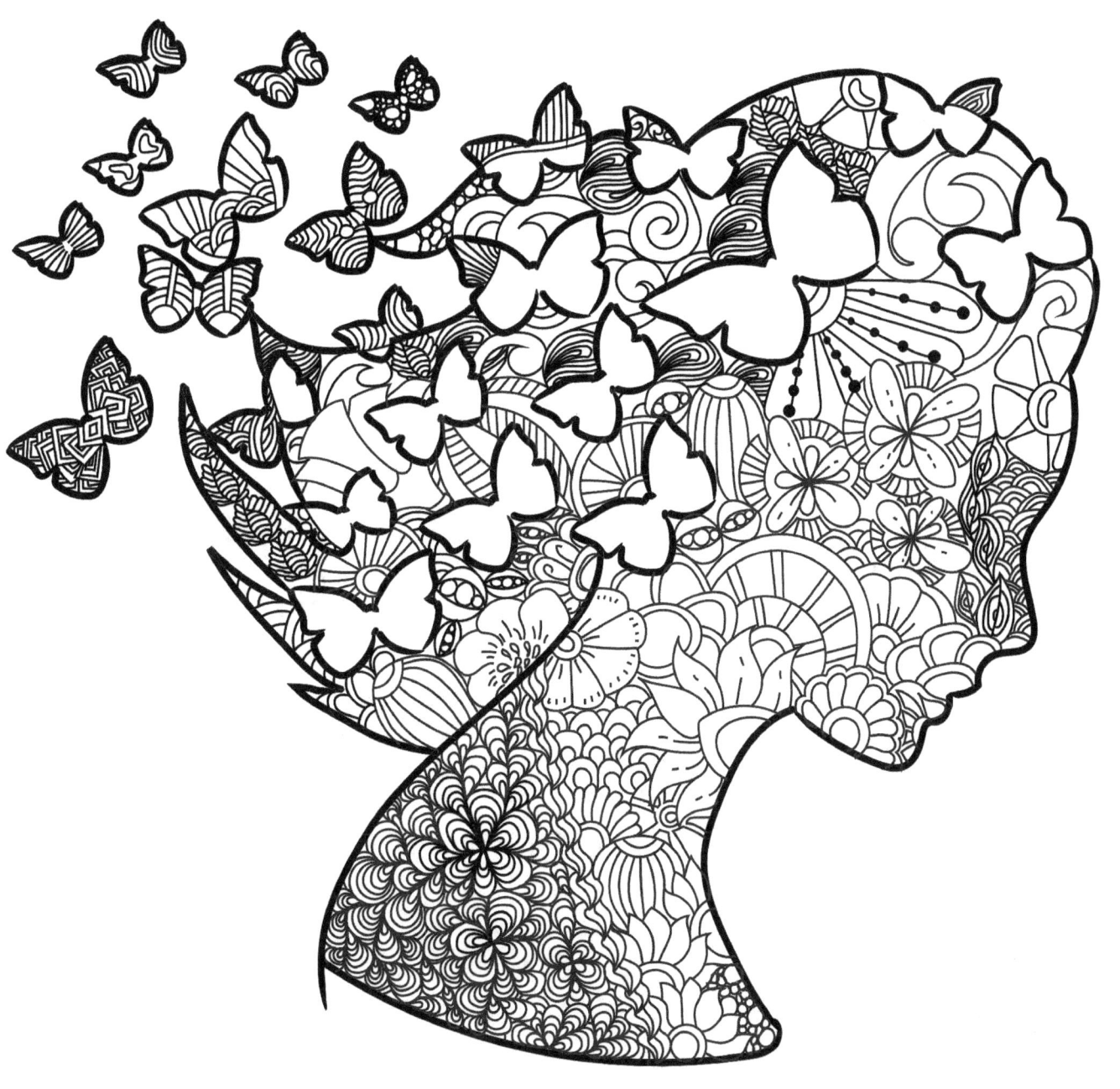

DONE is BETTER than PERFECT.

SHERYL SANDBERG
COO OF FACEBOOK

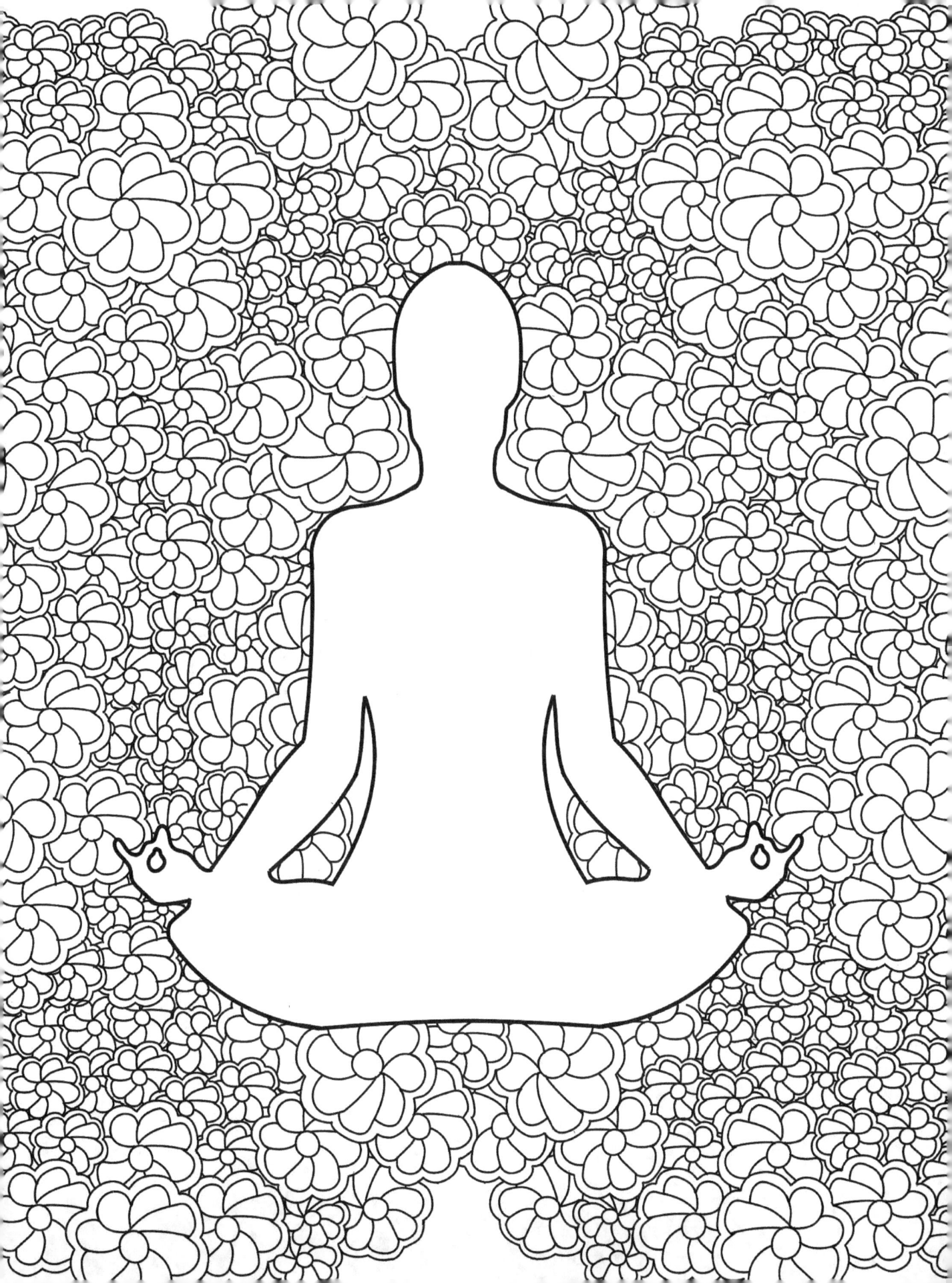

in order to be
irreplaceable, one must
always be
DIFFERENT

COCO CHANEL
FOUNDER OF THE CHANEL BRAND

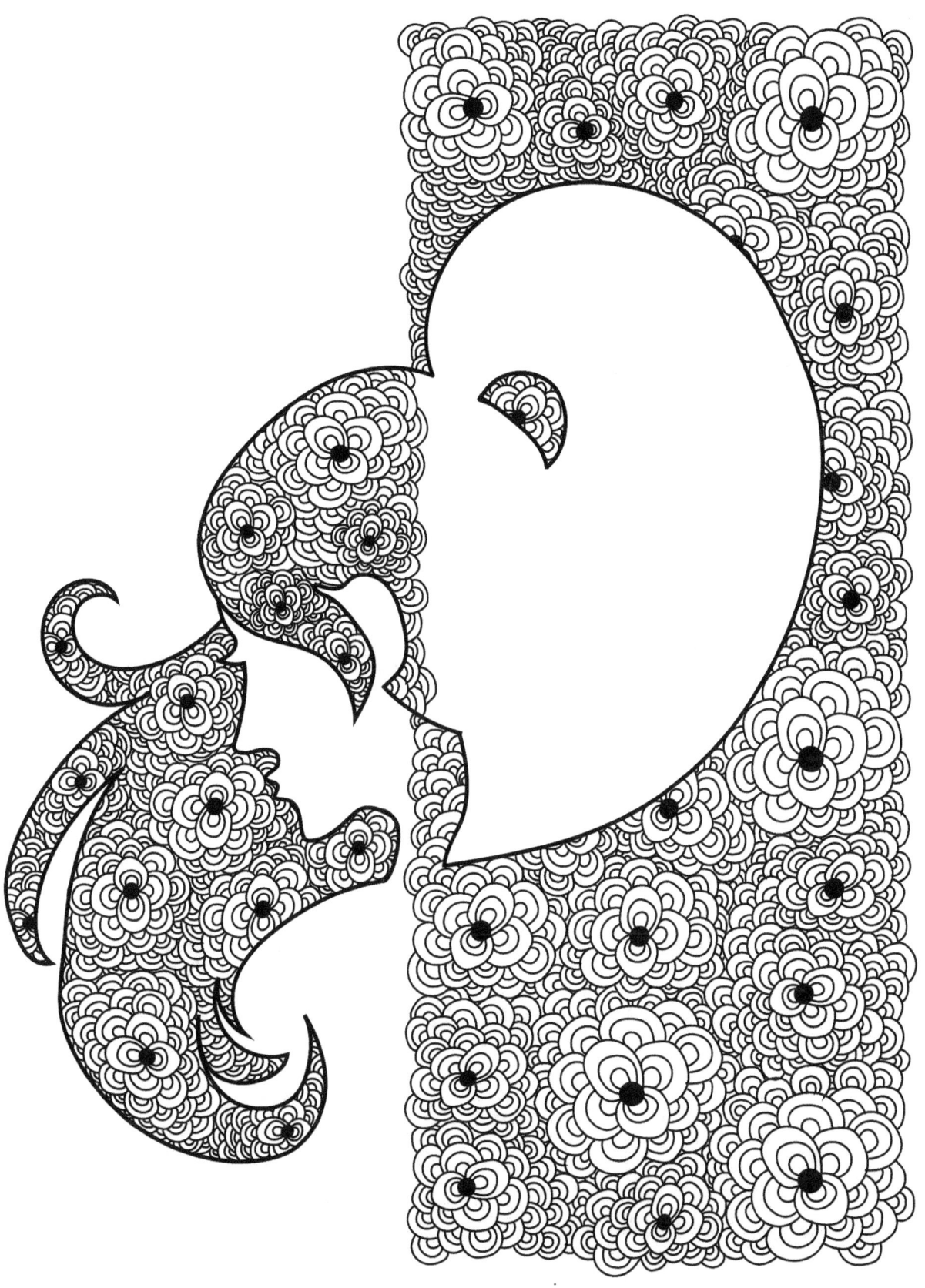

NORMAL is NOT something to aspire to, it's something to GET AWAY from.

JODIE FOSTER
AMERICAN ACTOR, DIRECTOR AND PRODUCER
ONE OF THE BEST ACTRESSES OF HER
GENERATION

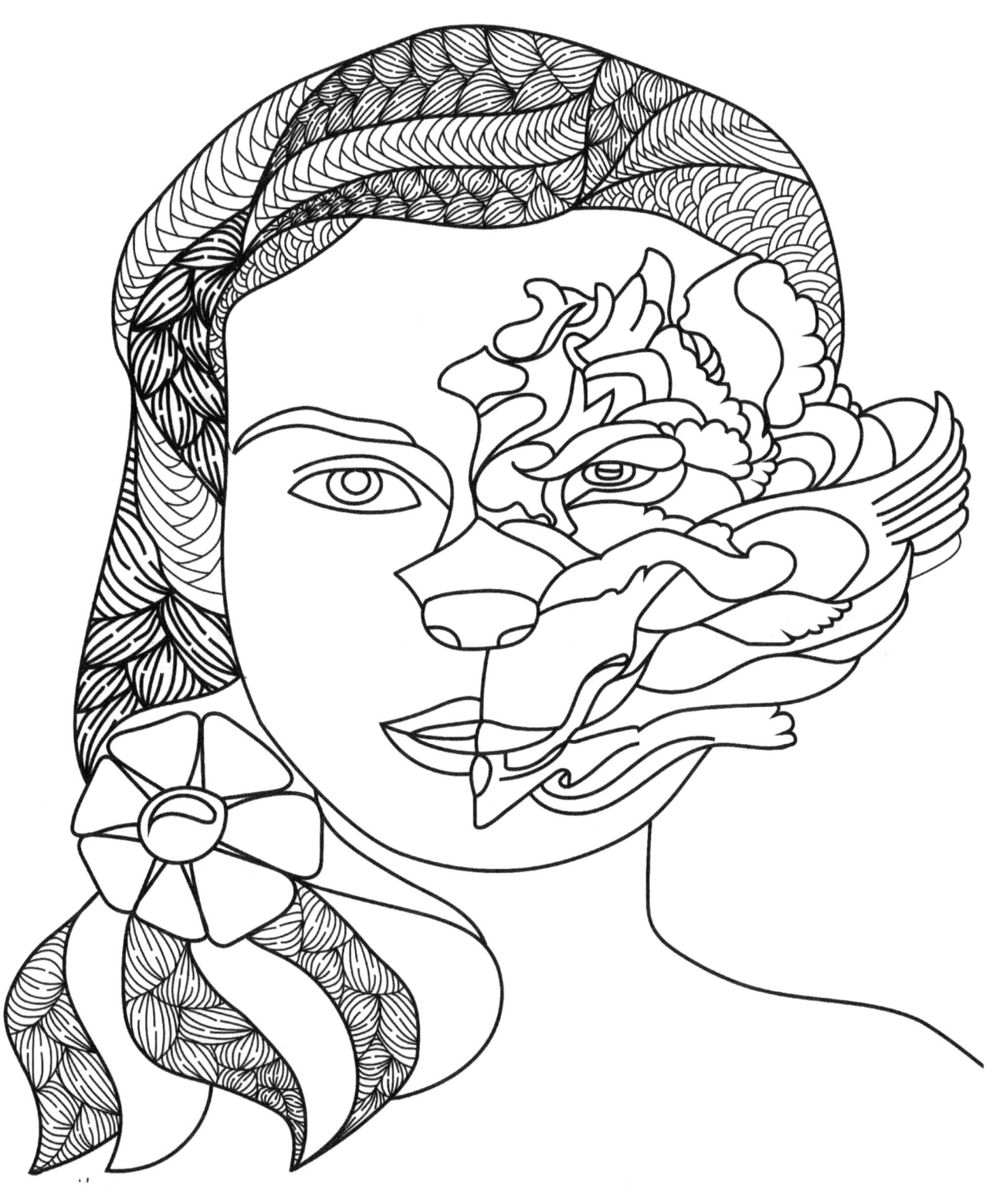

It's NOT the absence of FEAR, it's OVERCOMING it.

EMMA WATSON
BRITISH ACTRESS, MODEL, AND ACTIVIST

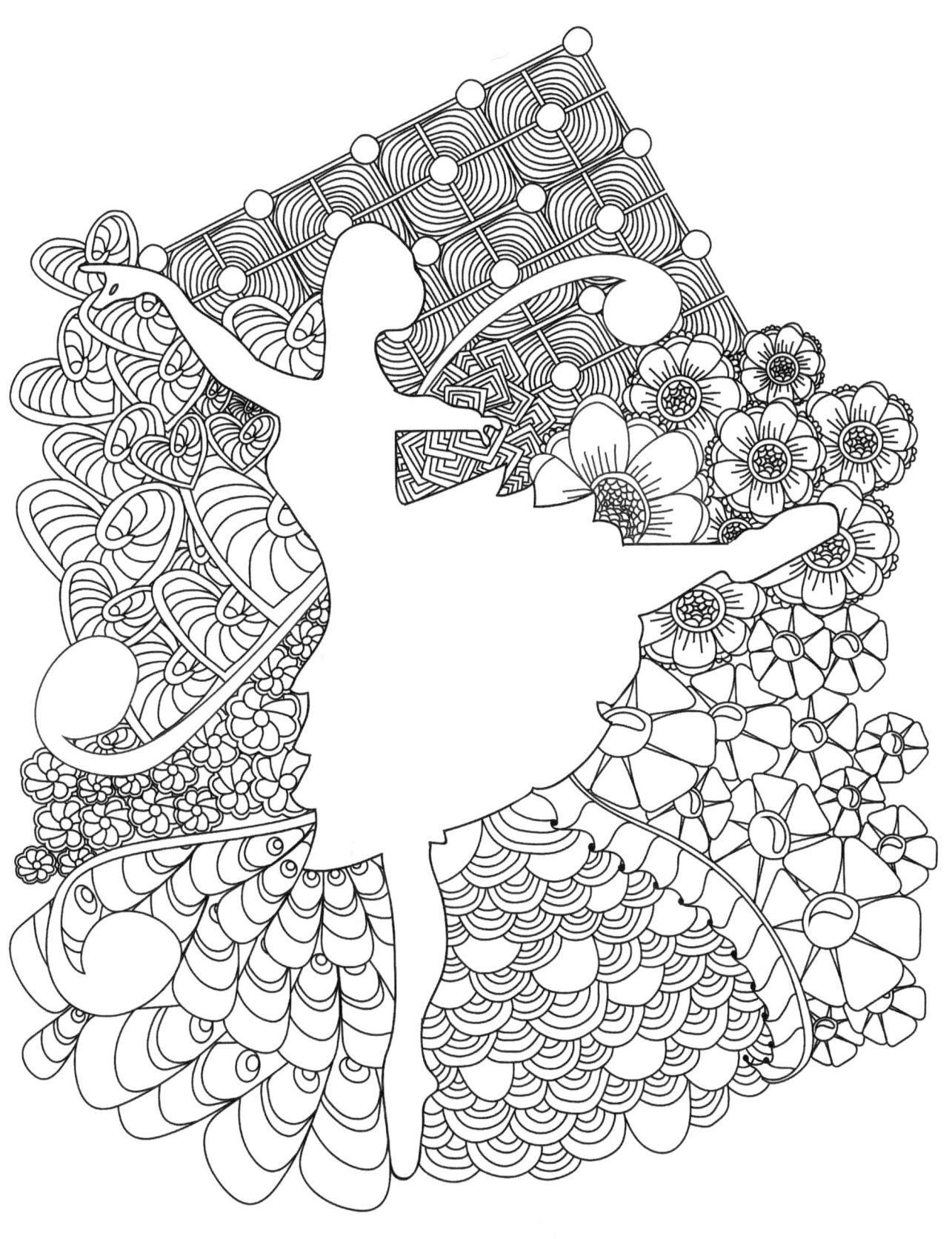

what you spend years
building, may be
DESTROYED overnight;
BUILD IT ANYWAY.

MOTHER TERESA
ROMAN CATHOLIC RELIGIOUS SISTER
AND MISSIONARY